THE DIGITAL WORLD

LEARN THE LANGUAGE OF

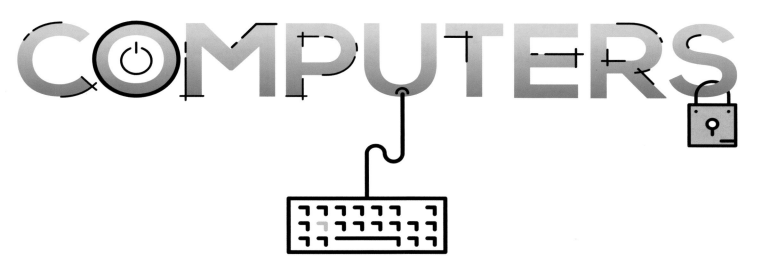

COMPUTERS

BY WILLIAM ANTHONY

Enslow
PUBLISHING

Published in 2022 by Enslow Publishing, LLC
101 W. 23rd Street, Suite 240
New York, NY 10011

Cataloging-in-Publication Data

Names: Anthony, William.
Title: Learn the language of computers / William Anthony.
Description: New York : Enslow Publishing, 2022. |
Series: The digital world
Identifiers: ISBN 9781978524750 (pbk.) | ISBN
9781978524774 (library bound) | ISBN 9781978524767
(6 pack) | ISBN 9781978524781 (ebook)
Subjects: LCSH: Computer science--Juvenile literature. |
Coding theory--Juvenile literature.
Classification: LCC QA76.23 W555 2022 | DDC 004--dc23

Designer: Dan Scase
Editor: Madeline Tyler

Printed in the United States of America

CPSIA compliance information: Batch #BSENS22: For further information contact
Enslow Publishing, New York, New York at 1-800-398-2504

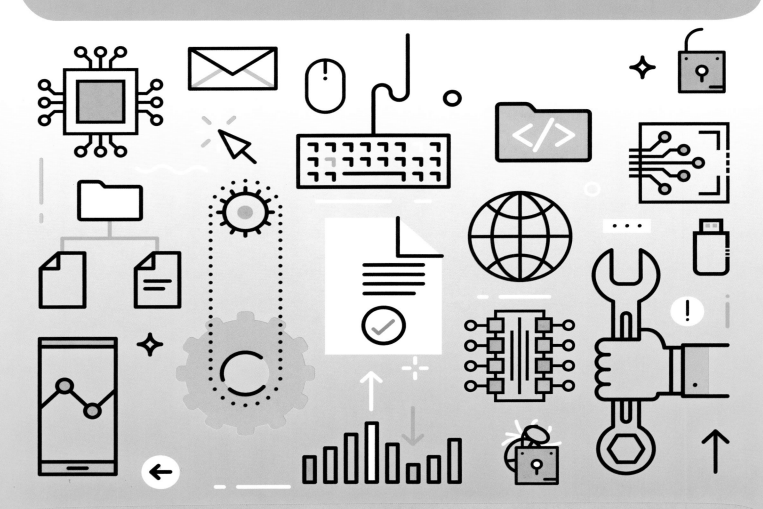

PHOTO CREDITS

All images are courtesy of Shutterstock.com, unless otherwise specified. With thanks to Getty Images, Thinkstock Photo, and iStockphoto.
Front Cover – Julia Kopacheva, jjjomathaidesigners. 4 – Macrovector, buffaloboy, drvector. 5 – Atstock Productions. 6 – Yes – Royalty Free, SkillUp,
Santitep Mongkolsin. 7 – hvostik, ShadeDesign, MchlSkhrv. 8 – Macrovector, Creative Stall, Shutterstock Vectorl. 9 – Vitya_M, pambudi, Martial Red. 10 –
KittyVector, sakmeniko, VectorsMarket. 11 – notbad, Fine Art. 12 – Alex Leo, vector toon. 13 – emre topdemir. 14 – T. Lesia, Tartila, Giamportone. 15 – Tetiana
Yurchenko, best4u, Mikhail Petrishchev. 16 – Pogorelova Olga, Martial Red. 17 – MMvector, Rauf Aliyev, bearsky23. 18 – Jane Kelly, andrerosi, StudioMark.
19 – VectorPot, Jane Kelly, Vector Market, iconvectorstock. 20 – illustratioz, BARS graphics. 21 – Ben Romalis. 22 – EgudinKa, Jane Kelly. 23 – M-vector,
Kyryloff, Oleg and Polly. 24 – Yurii Loud. 25 – MicroOne, WonderSTudio, Maksim M. 26 – AVIcon, Hilch, MOHAMMED ANOWAR HOSSAIN. 27– popicon,
Nice Illustration, XVector icon, Venomous Vector, Botond1977. 28 – icon99, Rauf Aliyev, popicon. 29 – linear_design, veronchick84. 30 – I musmellow,
T-Kot, Yuriy Vlasenko. 31 – wormig, mStudioVector, 4zevar, In-Finity.

HOW TO UNDERSTAND THE LANGUAGE OF COMPUTERS

Computers are complicated machines, and that's before you've even tried to learn the strange words that go with them. This handy guide will help you learn them all – but first, let's take a look at how to read each definition.

MEGAHERTZ
(MEGA-HURTS)

Noun: the measure of how fast your computer, or your CPU, is. It uses the abbreviation MHz. See **CPU**.

HEADWORD: this shows you how a word is spelled. These words are in alphabetical order.

PRONUNCIATION GUIDE: this tells you how to say a word. Say each part how it's written to pronounce the word correctly.

Word class: this is the type of word that the headword is. In this book you will see some of these:
- Noun – a person, place, or thing
- Verb – an action word
- Adjective – a describing word

Abbreviations: this is the type of word that the headword is. In this book you will see some of these:
- Initialism – a set of letters taken from several words that are read as individual letters
- Acronym – a set of letters taken from several words that make a new word

Definition: this is what the headword means.

RELATED WORDS: this shows you other words that link to the one you're looking at.

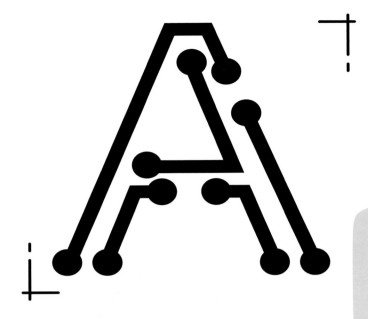

ALGORITHM

Noun: a set of instructions that a computer follows in the order that they have been given.

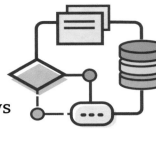

ACCESSIBILITY
(AK-SESS-IH-BIL-IH-TEE)

Adjective: how well and to what degree a device can be used, no matter what the user's abilities or disabilities are. For example, technology can be used to make computers more accessible for people with physical disabilities.

AI (Artificial Intelligence)

Initialism: machines with the ability to carry out tasks that normally require humans.

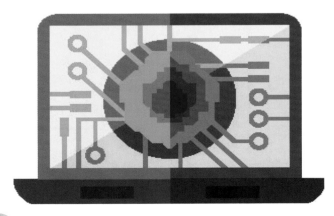

ANTIVIRUS PROTECTION
(AN-TEE-VY-RUS PRO-TEK-SHUN)

Noun: software that helps keep your computer, and the information stored on it, safe. See **VIRUS**.

APP

Noun: short for application. An app is a program installed and used on a computer system or portable device. Types of apps include games, internet browsers, and social media sites. See **BROWSER**.

ATTACHMENT

Noun: a document or file, such as an image or video, that is sent along with something else, such as an email. See **EMAIL**.

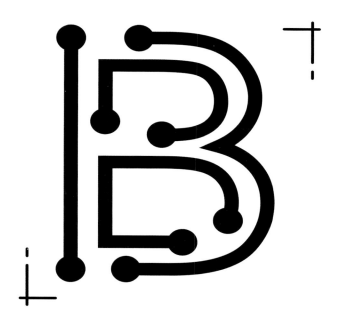

BACKGROUND

Noun: an image that is used behind icons and widgets on your desktop.
See **DESKTOP** and **WIDGET**.

BACKUP

Noun: a copy of a file or other item of data made in case the original is lost or damaged. See **FILE**.

BANDWIDTH

Noun: how much data can be sent at once. Imagine two hoses, one thin and one thick. Both deliver water, but the bigger hose delivers more water at once – this is similar to how bandwidth works. The more bandwidth a connection has, the more data it can send and receive at one time. See **DATA**.

BETA
(BAY-TUH)

Noun: a version of software that is nearly complete. It is open to a small number of users to find bugs or problems before it goes live.

BINARY
(BYE-NAIR-EE)

Noun: the language that computers use. It is made up of a series of 1s and 0s.

```
01000010
01001001
01001110
01000001
01010010
01011001
00100000
01000011
01001111
01000100
01000101
```

BIT

Noun: a binary digit (0 or 1). This is the smallest unit of digital information.

BLUETOOTH

Noun: a wireless connection that can be used to transfer data, such as photos and videos, between devices over short distances.

BOOT

Verb: to start up a computer.

BOT

Noun: a program that is made to behave like a real person online and can interact with a system or user.

BROWSER

Noun: a computer program that is used to find and look at information on the internet. See **INTERNET**.

BUFFERING

Verb: downloading a certain amount of data before starting to play some music or a movie.

BUG

Noun: an error in a piece of software that stops it from working the way that it should.

BYTE
(BITE)

Noun: a unit of digital information that contains eight bits, which is stored in a computer. See **BIT**.

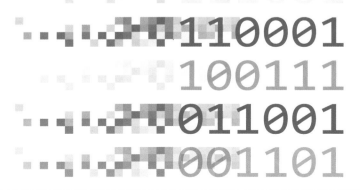

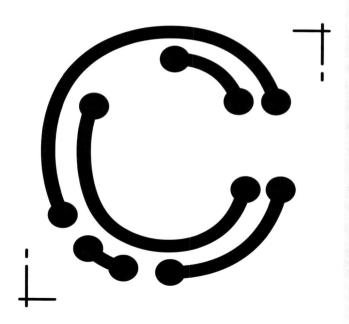

CACHE
(CASH)

Noun: a place where computers can store recently used information so that it can be accessed quickly the next time that it's needed.

CHATBOT

Noun: a type of bot that can be found in a messaging app and uses prompts to simulate a conversation. Lots of companies use these to talk to customers if they don't have enough employees available. See **BOT**.

CHIP

Noun: a small computer component, also known as a microchip, that processes information.

CLOUD

Noun: the large computers, called servers, that you can connect to on the internet and use for storing data. See **SERVERS**.

CODE

Noun: the language that programmers create and use to tell a computer what to do.

CODING

Verb: putting information and commands into a program to create software, apps, and websites.

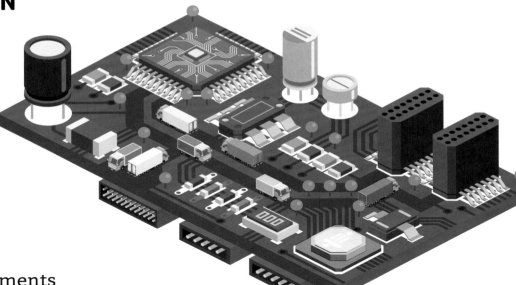

COMMUNICATION TECHNOLOGY

Noun: equipment that we use to communicate, such as a computer, cell phone, or tablet.

COMPONENTS

Noun: parts or elements that make up a system or object and perform specific tasks.

COPY AND PASTE

Verb: to take information from one place, such as the internet, and put it in another, such as a text document.

CPU (Central Processing Unit)

Initialism: like the brain of the computer. When people talk about the speed of a computer they are talking about the speed of the CPU.

CRASH

Verb: when your computer temporarily stops working. It may freeze or tell you to restart or quit. See **FREEZE**.

CURSOR

Noun: the pointer controlled by moving your mouse or using your touchpad. It shows you what you're hovering or clicking on. See **MOUSE**.

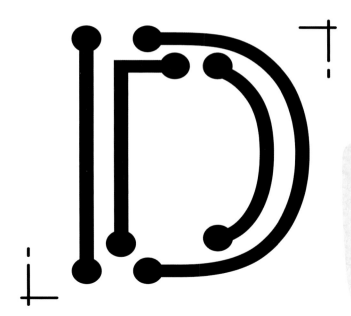

DATA
Noun: information that can be understood by a computer, such as text, images, and videos.

DATABASE
Noun: a set of data held in a computer that can be organized and used in lots of different ways. See **DATA**.

DEFAULT
Adjective: the original settings that a system or program starts with. You can usually reset your custom settings to their default. See **SETTINGS**.

WORD RUSH

There are a lot of words in this book, but how many of them can you make from these letters in just 2 minutes? You can use each letter square just once for each word. Play on your own or grab a friend to challenge. Find a pen, get some paper, and start the timer! 3... 2... 1...

L	E	C	T	I	A
W	D	H	U	Y	R
S	B	Z	A	P	O
J	E	K	M	Q	D
I	N	I	T	R	E
U	F	A	V	G	N

DESKTOP

Noun: the area where different program shortcuts are pinned on a screen, which is similar to how you might lay out documents and photos on a real desk. Users can decide how they want their desktop organized.

DEVELOPER

Noun: someone who is involved in coding or programming a computer or a piece of software. See **CODING** and **SOFTWARE**.

DOCUMENT

Noun: an electronic file created by a program that may contain text, images, audio, video, or any other type of data. See **FILE**.

DONGLE

Noun: a small device, such as a USB stick, that you can connect to your computer to do a particular task, such as provide access to a wireless internet connection.

DOWNLOAD

Verb: to copy data from one computer system to another, usually across the internet. See **INTERNET**.

DRIVER

Noun: a piece of software a computer uses to communicate with hardware such as printers and scanners. See **HARDWARE** and **SOFTWARE**.

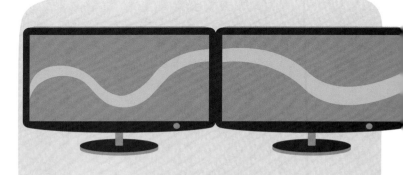

DUAL MONITORS

Noun: two displays that work together on a computer to extend the screen space available to the user.

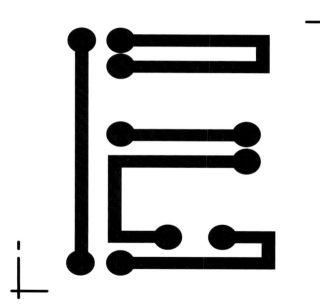

EMAIL

Noun: electronic messages that can be sent from one device to another over the internet. See **INTERNET**.

ENCRYPTION
(EN-CRIP-SHUN)

Noun: a way of changing and scrambling information so that it can't be read by anyone who doesn't know the password or key to unscramble it. This makes the information safer.

ERROR

Noun: a message letting you know that something has gone wrong or is not working as it should.

ETHERNET CABLE
(EE-THER-NET CAY-BUL)

Noun: a wire used to connect devices to each other or to the internet. If your Wi-Fi connection isn't working and you need to access the internet, you might have to use an ethernet cable to connect your computer to your router. See **ROUTER** and **WI-FI**.

EXPORT

Verb: to send a finished project to the computer to be saved as a file.

A B C D E F G H I J K L M N O P Q R S T U V W X Y Z

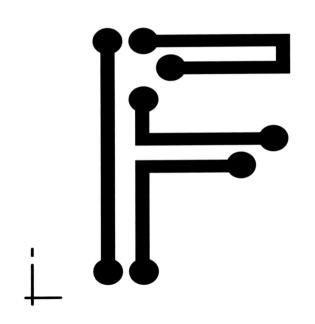

FILE

Noun: a collection of data stored in one place under a chosen name. This could be a video, an image, or a text document.

FILE NOT FOUND

Noun: a message that means your computer or web browser can't find the file that you've asked it to look for.

FLASH

Noun: a plug-in used to create and play interactive videos, games, and other multimedia items on the internet. See **PLUG-IN**.

FACTORY RESET

Noun: a feature that allows you to return your device to the exact settings it had when it came out of the box. BE CAREFUL! This wipes all the saved data and information from your device.

FAN

Noun: a piece of hardware that keeps a computer cool by creating an airflow inside the system. See **HARDWARE**.

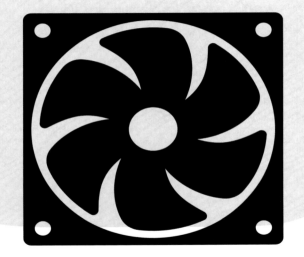

FOLDER

Noun: a place to store and organize computer files. A folder is given a name so that it can be easily found.

FREEZE

Verb: when a computer stops loading, moving, or working correctly. If you're on a website, try refreshing the page to correct it. If it's your whole computer that's frozen, try the oldest trick in the book: turn it off and on again. See **TIOAOA**.

32167
220
6G

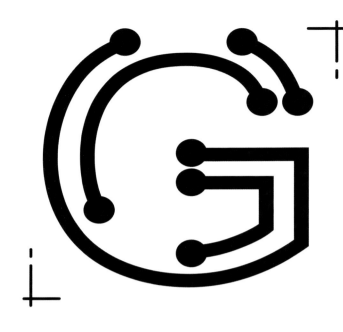

GPU
(Graphics Processing Unit)
Initialism: hardware that sends images to the computer screen for the user to see.
See **HARDWARE**.

GRAPHICS CARD
(GRA-FICKS CARD)
Noun: a piece of hardware that helps a computer to display high-quality images such as those used in games and videos.

GIGABYTE
(GIH-GUH-BITE)
Noun: a unit of data equal to 1,000 megabytes. See **MEGABYTE**.

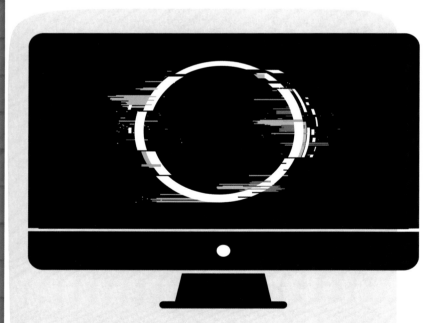

GLITCH
Noun: when something in a computer does not work correctly, causing a problem.

GUI (Graphical User Interface)
Initialism: the things that the user can see and touch or click on. See **USER INTERFACE**.

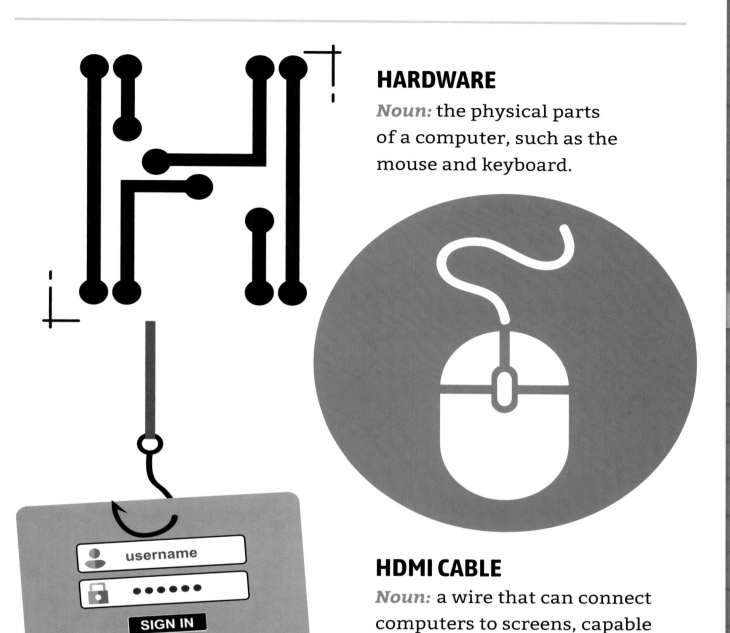

HARDWARE
Noun: the physical parts of a computer, such as the mouse and keyboard.

HDMI CABLE
Noun: a wire that can connect computers to screens, capable of carrying HD and 4K signals.

HEAT SINK
Noun: a piece of equipment designed to take heat away from the computer's processor to stop it from overheating. See **PROCESSOR**.

HACK
Verb: to break into a computer system to find problems with the code, or to cause harm to the computer. See **CODE**.

username

SIGN IN

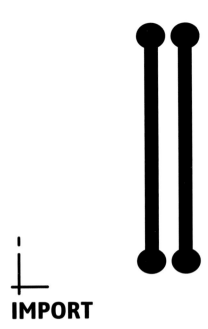

IMPORT

Verb: to bring something into a program from something outside it.
See **PROGRAM**.

INPUT

Noun: data that is entered into a computer from hardware such as a mouse or a keyboard.
See **HARDWARE.**

INSTALL

Verb: to transfer software onto your computer and set it up so that it can work properly.
See **SOFTWARE.**

INTERNET

Noun: a system that connects computers throughout the world.
See **WORLD WIDE WEB**.

INTRANET

Noun: a private network of computers that can only be accessed by specific people.
See **NETWORK.**

IP ADDRESS

Noun: a number assigned to a computer that is connected to the internet, which will look something like "01.234.56.789." It helps to locate where in the world the computer is.

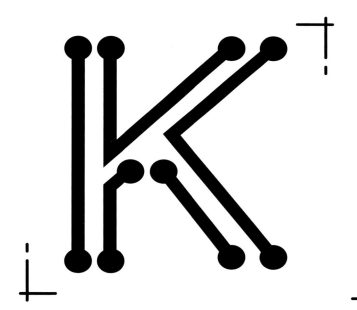

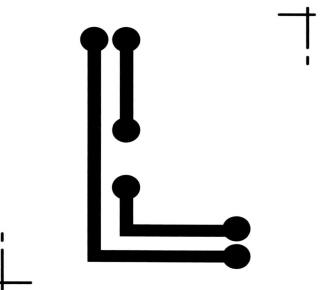

KEYBOARD

Noun: a set of keys that are used for a computer. Most keys have at least a letter, a number, a word, or a symbol on them.

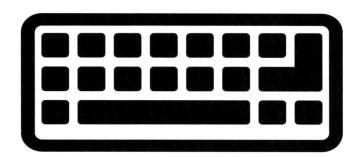

KILOBYTE
(KIH-LOW-BITE)

Noun: a unit of data equal to 1,024 bytes. See **BYTE**.

LAPTOP

Noun: a small, foldable personal computer that combines a screen, keyboard, and trackpad in an easy-to-carry format. See **PC**.

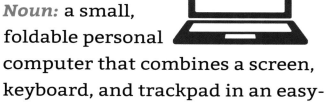

LINK

Noun: a virtual bridge from one website to another, to direct people somewhere, or to allow information to be shared.

LOGGING ON/OFF

Verb: entering and exiting a computer account by using your details and a password. When sharing a computer, always log off of all your accounts when you are done so no one else has access to them.

\# A B C D E F G H I J K L M N O P Q R S T U V W X Y Z

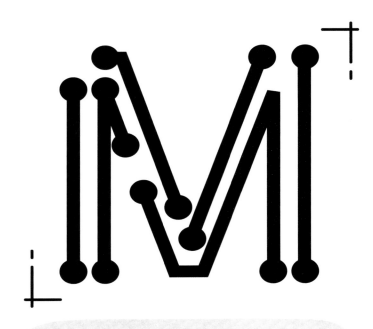

MEDIA

Noun: ways of communicating information. This could be through writing, photos, videos, or audio, among others.

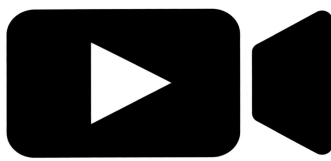

MALWARE

Noun: harmful software designed to mess with the normal operation of a computer. See **SOFTWARE**.

MEGABYTE

Noun: a unit of data equal to 1,000 kilobytes. See **KILOBYTE**.

MEGAHERTZ
(MEGA-HURTS)

Noun: the measure of how fast your computer, or your CPU, is. It uses the abbreviation MHz. See **CPU**.

MEMORY STICK

Noun: a small piece of hardware that you can plug into your computer through a USB port to store data. See **USB**.

MANUFACTURER

Noun: a person or company that makes things to be sold.

MENU

Noun: a list of options available.

MONITOR

Noun: the electronic display for your computer. It's the part you look at!

MOTHERBOARD

Noun: the main part of a computer. Everything inside the computer connects to this.

MP3

Noun: a type of audio file that can be downloaded and stored on devices, which allows people to listen to music.

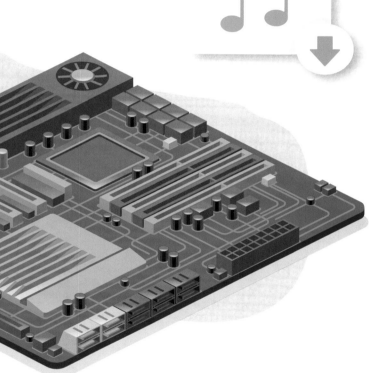

MOUSE

Noun: a small device that is connected to a computer. You move the mouse with your hand to control the movement of a cursor on the computer screen. See **CURSOR**.

MULTIMEDIA

Noun: combinations of text, graphics, video, animation, and/or sound. See **MEDIA**.

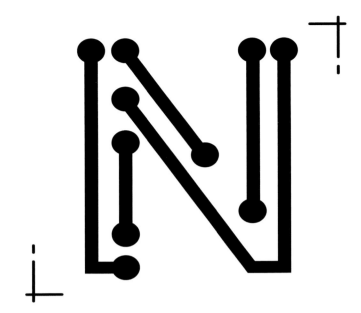

NETWORK

Noun: computers and devices within a building or area that are linked together.

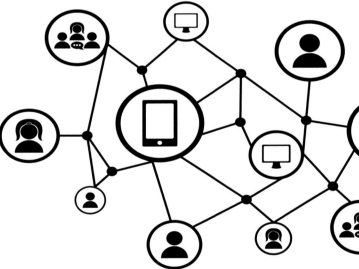

NOTEBOOK

Noun: a very small and very thin type of laptop. They weigh less and are thinner than a regular laptop.

OFFLINE

Adjective: when your device isn't connected to the internet.

ONLINE

Adjective: when your device is connected to the internet, and the World Wide Web is ready at your fingertips. See **WORLD WIDE WEB**.

OPERATING SYSTEM

Noun: the main program in a computer that controls the way the device works and makes it possible for other programs to function.

OUTPUT

Noun: information that comes out of the computer.

OVERHEATING

Verb: when a computer produces too much heat, causing it to stop working.

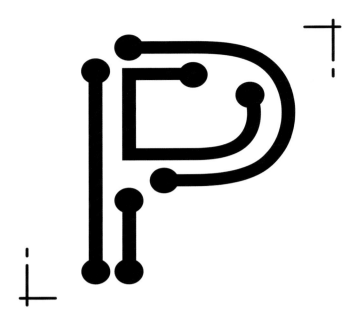

PDF
(Portable Document Format)

Initialism: a type of file that captures electronic documents in exactly the way they were intended to be seen.

PDF

PASSWORD

Noun: a secret combination of letters, numbers, and characters that protects personal information.

PATH

Noun: the location of a file or folder on your computer system. See **FOLDER**.

PIXELS

Noun: the tiny units of a digital image. When you look at a picture on a screen, you are looking at a collection of hundreds, thousands, or even hundreds of thousands of tiny colored dots.

PC (Personal Computer)

Initialism: a piece of hardware that can process and understand bits of data stored as 1s and 0s. See **HARDWARE**.

PLUG-AND-PLAY

Adjective: hardware that doesn't have to be installed before you can use it on your computer. You can plug it in and use it right away.

PLUG-IN

Noun: an extra bit of software code, such as Flash, that needs to be added to your browser before you can view or use certain types of content. See **FLASH**.

PRINTER

Noun: a machine that is used for printing documents and photographs, among other things.

PROCESSOR

Noun: the computer chip inside a computer that is used to run programs.

PROGRAM

Noun: a collection of instructions or algorithms designed to make processes simple. See **ALGORITHM**.

PUSH NOTIFICATION

Noun: an automatic message sent to your computer by an app, even when the app isn't open. See **APP**.

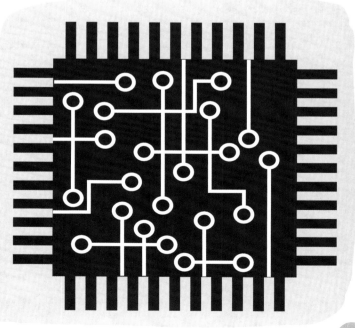

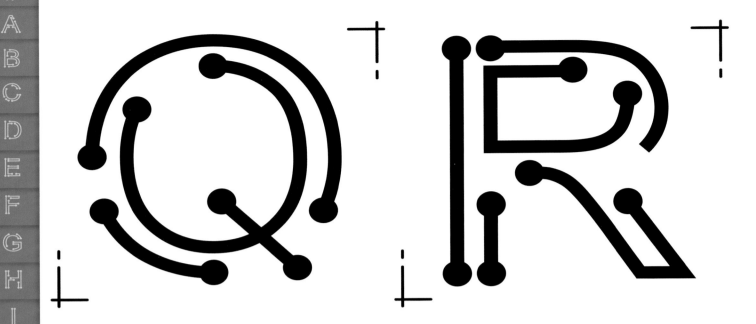

QR CODE

Noun: a square with lots of smaller square and rectangular shapes inside that can be scanned by a device and used to launch a website.

QWERTY KEYBOARD

Noun: a layout of keyboard in which the first six letters on the top row spell QWERTY. This is where it gets its name. See **KEYBOARD**.

RAM (Random Access Memory)

Acronym: the amount of "thinking memory" your computer has to perform lots of different tasks quickly.

REBOOT

Verb: to turn off a computer and then immediately turn it on. See **TIOAOA**.

REMOTE DESKTOP

Noun: a program that allows someone to use or log on to a computer from somewhere far away from it.

RGB (Red Green Blue)

Initialism: a way of creating color, displayed on pixels, through the use of different amounts of red, green, and blue light. Any color can be created by combining these three colors. See **PIXELS**.

RIGHT-CLICK

Verb: pressing the button on the right of some mice or trackpads in order to open a menu. The menu is related to the thing you have clicked on.

ROUTER
(ROU-TUHR)

Noun: a piece of hardware that directs wireless signals, such as an internet connection, to other electronic devices. Try turning this off and on again if your internet signal has stopped. See **WI-FI** and **TIOAOA**.

WORD SEARCH

L	E	T	A	A	B	P	F
Z	A	P	E	T	A	I	I
I	F	I	L	E	T	X	L
B	S	X	T	R	O	T	B
E	F	E	O	M	P	Z	O
T	Y	L	Z	F	I	I	T
A	C	S	D	I	X	B	J
F	A	L	E	L	P	H	G

Can you spot some of the words from this book in a crowd of letters? Do this word search and see if you can find every one!

- BETA
- BOT
- FILE
- PIXELS
- ZIP

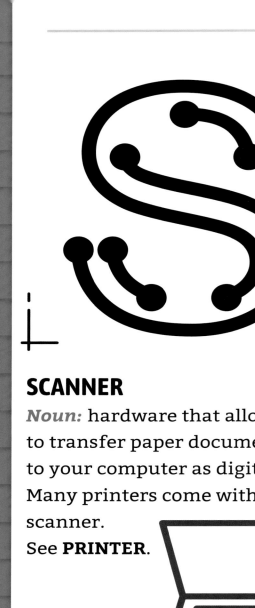

SCANNER

Noun: hardware that allows you to transfer paper documents on to your computer as digital files. Many printers come with a built-in scanner.
See **PRINTER**.

SCREENSAVER

Noun: a program that plays moving images or patterns when a screen is not in use. This was used to stop screen burn-in, where an image is permanently "burned" into a screen. Modern screens use them for security or privacy.

SCREENSHOT

Noun: an image taken of whatever is on a device's screen.

SERVERS

Noun: computers used for storing files that can be accessed by the network. See **NETWORK**.

SETTINGS

Noun: an application or menu that lets you customize the way a device looks or behaves.

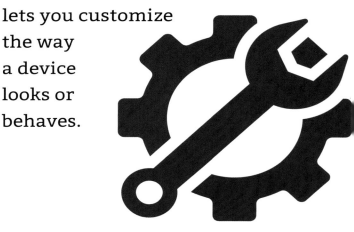

SHORTCUT

Noun: an icon that makes it quicker and easier to get to a document, file, or program.

SOFTWARE

Noun: programs that run on a computer and control how it works.

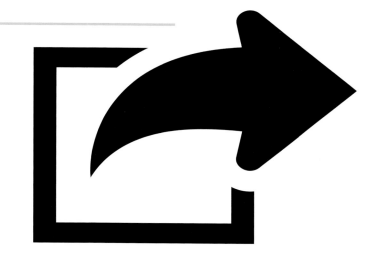

STREAMING

Verb: watching a video file or listening to a music file at almost the same time that it is being downloaded by your computer. This way, you don't have to wait for it to be downloaded first.

SOUND CARD

Noun: a piece of hardware in a computer that allows you to listen to sound.

SUBFOLDER

Noun: a folder contained inside another folder. See **FOLDER**.

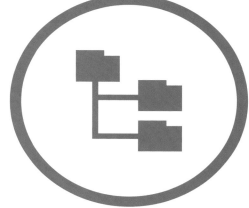

A B C D E F G H I J K L M N O P Q R S T U V W X Y Z

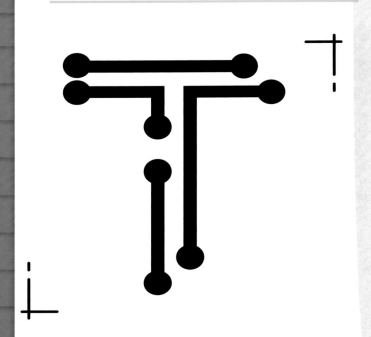

TIOAOA (Turn It Off and On Again)

Initialism: the first, and usually most successful, solution to fixing a computer that is behaving badly. This is usually the go-to suggestion when you call IT departments.

TERABYTE
(TEH-RUH-BITE)

Noun: a unit of data equal to 1,000 gigabytes. See **GIGABYTE**.

TRACKPAD

Noun: a small and smooth surface on a laptop that is used instead of a mouse. See **MOUSE**.

TETHERING
(TETH-ER-ING)

Noun: the linking of one device to another in order to share an internet connection.

TROJAN

Noun: a program that appears harmless but is carrying viruses or even other programs within it that will damage your computer or allow someone to hack into it. See **HACK**.

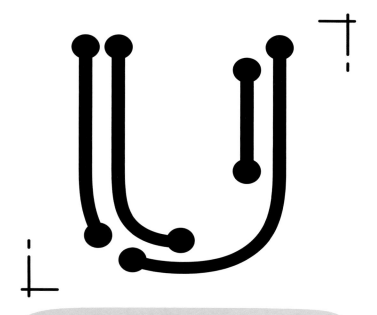

USB (Universal Serial Bus)

Initialism: a system for connecting a device to a computer.

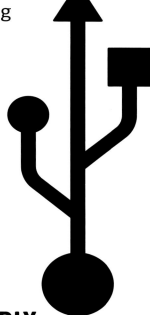

UPDATE

Noun: a change or addition to computer software that includes the most recent information. See **SOFTWARE**.

UPLOAD

Verb: to copy data from your computer system to another, usually across the internet.

USER-FRIENDLY

Adjective: a type of program that is built in an easy-to-use way.

USER-GENERATED CONTENT

Noun: information or media created for the internet by the people who use it. This might be in the form of videos, blogs, photos, and much more.

USER INTERFACE

Noun: the way a user can interact with a computer, and the options they are given to do so.

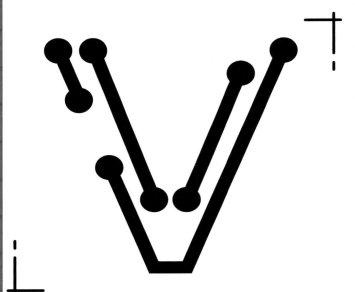

VIRUS

Noun: a type of malware that multiplies to spread across multiple computers and affects how they perform. See **MALWARE**.

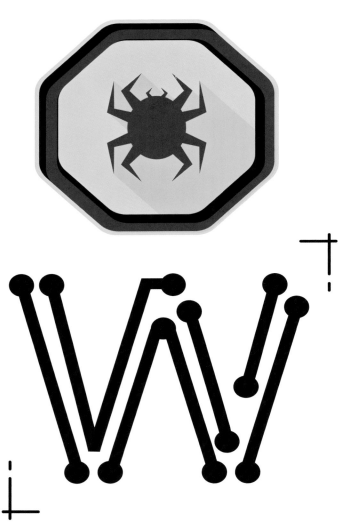

VGA (Video Graphics Array)

Initialism: the standard type of display connection for most PCs. See **PC**.

VIDEO CALL

Noun: a type of call that allows you to see the other person

or people through their camera.

VIDEO CARD

Noun: a piece of hardware inside a computer that allows you to view high-quality video files.

WEBCAM

Noun: a small camera that is either built into or can be plugged into your computer so that you can see and talk to people over the internet. You should only use a webcam to talk to people you know.

See **VIDEO CALL**.

WIDGET
(WIH-JIT)
Noun: a fancy shortcut that lets you use certain features of an app without completely opening the app. See **APP**.

WI-FI
(WHY-FY)
Noun: a facility that lets computers, smartphones, or other devices connect to the internet.

WIRELESS DEVICE
Noun: a device that sends and receives data from other places without using any wires. A common example of a wireless device is a laptop.

WORLD WIDE WEB
Noun: a collection of web pages found on the internet.

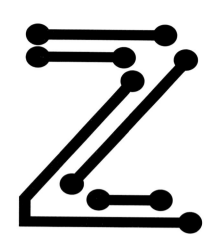

ZIP
Noun: a file that has been compressed to hold lots of information without taking up lots of storage. ZIP files are much easier to transfer over the internet than larger folders. See **FOLDER**.

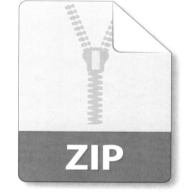

ZOMBIE COMPUTER
Noun: a computer that someone has hacked into over the internet and can be used to do whatever the hacker wants without the owner noticing.

A B C D E F G H I J K L M N O P Q R S T U V W X Y Z

WORD MATCH

Now that you've learned all the words in this book, can you match them up to the correct definitions? Can you complete them all without looking back at the rest of the book?

TERMS

- **EXPORT**
- **MEGABYTE**
- **OFFLINE**
- **PROCESSOR**
- **ALGORITHM**
- **HARDWARE**
- **FOLDER**
- **BACKGROUND**
- **DATA**
- **CODE**
- **GIGABYTE**
- **TERABYTE**

DEFINITIONS

- a place to store and organize computer files
- a unit of data equal to 1,000 gigabytes
- the language that programmers create and use to tell a computer what to do
- information that can be understood by a computer, such as text, images, and videos
- send a finished project to the computer to be saved as a file
- a set of instructions that a computer follows in the order that they have been given
- a unit of data equal to 1,000 megabytes
- the physical parts of a computer, such as the mouse and keyboard
- a unit of data equal to 1,000 kilobytes
- an image that is used behind icons and widgets on your desktop
- the computer chip inside a computer that is used to run programs
- when your device isn't connected to the internet

A B C D E F G H I J K L M N O P Q R S T U V W X Y Z